"Ribbit," said the frog,
lost in the fog.

"Buzz!" said the Bee,
"Look at me!"

"Quack," said the duck,
"I am in luck!"

"Cheep," said the chick,
pecking at a stick.

"Whee!" said the wombat,
jumping off a hat.

"Woof," said the dog,
stuck in a log.

"Boing!" said the kangaroo,
"I can spring too."

"Ouch!" said the snail,
out in the hail.

"Oink!" said the pig,
"You are big!"

"Mmm," said the skunk,
sitting in the junk.

"Blob," said the fish,
and had a wish.

"Snap!" said the shark,
and that was that.